Photography: Ken Krakow
Cover Design: Mary Lee Irby
Graphic Design: Corry Dieh
Illustrator: Cindy Eversole

Ghosts
of Macon

Happy Haunting!
Catherine!

Mary Lee Irby

Ghosts
of Macon

Mary Lee Irby

Vestige Publishing Company, Inc. ~ Macon, Georgia

Mary Lee Irby ─────────────────────

Published by

Vestige Publishing Company, Inc.
P.O. Box 13726
Macon, Georgia 31208-3726

ISBN# 0-966682-8312

Library of Congress Card Catalog # 98-90472

For My Grandfather

"Grandy"

Willie P. Fullbright
May 14, 1899
December 29,1978

Who believed in me even at a young age.

Contents

Special Thanks

*T*here are numerous individuals who were instrumental in the creation of this publication. I wish to thank all of them for their part in making *Ghosts of Macon* possible. They include: my husband Bobby who supported and encouraged me throughout this unusual journey; my dear family, the Hicks and the Irbys, who always believed in me; Kathleen Thomason at Ingleside Books who advised me through the perils of publication; the gang at Ivan Allen Print Shop, especially Kelly, Corry and Cindy for their creative enthusiasm and belief in my project; local photographer Ken Krakow and his staff for taking or enhancing all of the photographs appearing in the book; Muriel, Willard and the staff at the Middle Georgia Archives, Washington Memorial Library, Macon, Georgia, for pointing me in the right direction and making their precious records so readily available; my numerous proofreaders and budding editors who attempted to make sure there were no mistakes; historical ghost authors Barbara Duffey and Nancy Roberts for their inspiration and support; the staff and residents of local landmarks for taking the time to share with me their experiences; and finally, the readers. My only hope is that you will enjoy reading this book half as much as I enjoyed writing it.

-Mary Lee Irby

Cover: Pen & Ink by F. S. Suddeth
Courtesy of Middle Georgia Archives,
Washington Memorial Library, Macon, Georgia

Marshall-Johnston Home
(Once located on Coleman Hill, Macon, Georgia)
1883-1954

This book is a tribute to the
Marshall-Johnston home
and other 19th century relics
no longer with us.

"All houses in which men have lived and died
Are haunted houses: through the open door
The harmless phantoms on their errands glide
With feet that make no sound upon the floor."

-Henry Wordsworth Longfellow
1807-1882

"People remembers it.
People forgets if it ain't
wrote down."

-From *All Over but the Shoutin'*
A Memoir by Rick Bragg

Preface

*F*or a city whose downtown is perched on the banks of the Ocmulgee and whose historic landmarks are prevalent everywhere you turn, it comes as no surprise that many, many ghost stories abound. Since moving to the area in 1992, I have been intrigued with Macon's history. Whether it was Ft. Hawkins, the Grand Opera House or the Ocmulgee Indian Mounds, I was curious for a glimpse into Macon's rich past. Historical tours and books are abundant, but what about the real people who lived here hundreds or even thousand of years ago yet sometimes seem to reappear today? Could traces of their lives have been so filled with emotion that they have superimposed themselves in time only to be replayed again?

On impulse, I began asking many at Macon's historical locations about their ghostly encounters. I sensed that spirits surely lurked somewhere in a town as beautiful and rich with Southern charm and history as Macon. One only needs to see the beautiful mixture of magnolia trees, azaleas and green hillsides coupled with the stark contrast of the beautiful historical homes of downtown to feel it.

During the journey on which this book has taken me, I have had the privilege of speaking with people of all walks of life, all ages and all backgrounds. They may or may not tell you they actually believe in ghosts, but once they warm up they usually always have an unexplained experience to share. It was after hearing many of these stories that I knew they had to be told.

I am always careful to say that this book is not an endorsement or confirmation of the supernatural but merely a romantic, historical look back at the Macon which use to be. Regardless if ghosts actually exist, they do have a very real place in the folklore and fiber of Macon's history. Whether you believe these tales is up to you. I am merely passing them along as they were told to me - for entertainment and historical purposes only. Enjoy!

-Mary Lee Irby
October, 1998

Introduction

*F*or over 10,000 years, Macon, Georgia has served as a focal point of the Southeastern region. Indian tribes were lured to the area thousands of years ago by the gently rising hills and a great red river called the Ocmulgee. It was from this sacred Native American territory that a frontier city filled with promise rose from the thick Georgia clay.

Founded in 1823, Macon has long continued to serve as a convenient trade and commercial center for Georgia and the Southeast. Located in the very center of the state and at the foothills of the Georgia Piedmont, Macon was once known as "The Seven Hilled City."

In the late 1800s, when the South was still licking its wounds from the civil war, cotton continued to be king in Macon with other industries also beginning to emerge. By the time Mercer and Wesleyan colleges arrived, many historic homes had already been built.

It is around these now historical dwellings and landmarks that this book is centered. Macon has housed a variety of souls throughout the years and has seen many come and go. Historical records and books may capture names and dates but what about the essence of day-to-day human life?

I have found that archives and old records will only speak to us if we listen. And others will only know if we tell. So take pride in a Macon past and present. I guarantee you will be in good company and you might even learn something, as I have, along the way.

Ghosts
of Macon

Photo: Leah Yetter

1998 exterior photo of the Bennett House.

Chapter 1

"Uncle Pliny Approves"
Bennett House
Circa 1902
990 Georgia Avenue

loud crash suddenly startled Susan and her guests. It was almost midnight on Christmas Eve and they were enjoying a nightcap by the fire before retiring. "What was that?" inquired the startled guests. "That," said Susan, "was Uncle Pliny."

Susan and Gilbert Bennett have quite a job on their hands. They are currently restoring their 15,000 square foot, turn of the century home on the corner of Georgia Avenue and Nesbitt Place. Both hope to return the house to its original state. Some old photos recently uncovered are helping them to recapture the home's former grandeur and shedding some light onto some mysterious episodes.

When I visited them to learn more about their mansion, I was impressed with their enthusiasm for their task. I found out that many guests of the Bennett's are intrigued not only by the Classic Revival architecture but also by the home's underground spring.

The five story Bennett home covers the water source that was once used to supply the Johnston-Felton-Hay House. The spring is housed on the lowest level of the home and shares what was formerly the carriage house and chauffeur's quarters. It is located directly under the front porch in a 50 foot circumference domed shape room. The spring pumps over 40 gallons of natural water a minute and hovers at a constant 58 degrees.

Apparently, the spring enabled the Johnstons to enjoy hot and cold water long before it was available to most. Eventually the spring was even used to feed the YMCA swimming pool. "It's been tested by the office of the city engineer and is absolutely pure water," said Susan.

The house and spring are now home to both Susan and Gilbert, but once served as the official location of his CPA office. Susan and Gilbert married in 1989. "We married by the fireplace in the front sitting room. That same weekend I moved·my things in, totally unaware anything unusual had ever happened here," recalls Susan.

Photo: Ken Krakow

1998 photo of underground spring beneath Bennett House.

It began as the dream home of Eugene and Mary Ayers Harris who purchased the property on a muggy summer day in June of 1902. Originally, the land was part of the William B. Johnston's (Johnston-Felton-Hay House) estate but had been sold several years prior. Mary Ayers Harris' father, Asher, was most likely the one who lovingly built the house for his daughter and her husband. It was probably the first dwelling to be built on the original Hay House estates. According to Susan, "You have to have a feel for the period to get a real understanding of what they were trying to do by building this magnificent home."

The couple resided there for only about four years before selling it to an attorney named Mansfield Pliny Hall and his wife Mamie. Mamie loved to move around but Pliny (pronounced "plen-ee") swore that if they moved once more, he would stop practicing law. Pliny was tired of trying to re-establish his clientele in every town they re-sided. Mamie won out and true to his word, Pliny quit his practice. They filled the house with love, laughter and parties and still make their presence known even today.

Uncle Pliny, as he is affectionately known, is not a bad spirit. Rather, Susan and Gilbert feel Mamie and Pliny are pleased at what they are trying to do with their former home. "Uncle Pliny was eccentric, yet a favorite among many in Macon. He loved to smoke a pipe, cook and go barefoot. He also loved the Hardeman Avenue Fire Sta-tion and continued some pro-bono legal work for them after he retired. We've found out that he would spend hours down there with the firemen talking and telling sto-ries," said Susan.

Gilbert's first encounter with Uncle Pliny came on a chilly, fall evening in November of 1976, two weeks after he had bought the home as his CPA office and residence. He was practicing his CPA business by day and sleeping in the house at night so he could begin the preliminary priming and painting. The second week he was staying in the house, about 2 o'clock in the morning, he was asleep down-stairs when he awoke to the sound of someone opening the front door. He heard a man's footfall as if someone was strolling across the entrance hall. Then he heard some-one open the door to the room where he was sleeping. Before he went to bed, he always secured both doors with special chains and locks. He immediately turned on the light to see who was in the room, but there was no one there. The door to his room was still locked and when he checked the front door, it remained locked and secured as well. He searched the house checking for an intruder but found himself alone. This baffled him but he decided to put it behind him and focus on his practice and new home.

The next incident occurred two years later in 1978, when Glibert's son was visiting. His son Steve, was working on his master's degree at the University of Alabama (his dad's alma mater) and was home for a brief stay. Father and son were sleeping in two of the upstairs bedrooms. About 2 o'clock in the morning, both were awakened by the sound of the front door opening and closing and a man, once again, casually walking across the front hall. They checked the house and turned on all the lights but no one was there. In fact, all the doors were still locked. It was strange because both had been awakened from a deep sleep at the same moment and heard the same thing.

Susan and Gilbert's courtship lasted eight years and yet she had never learned of either incident. Her first encounter occurred about a week after they were married. In fact, it centered around a simple visit from the telephone man. She said she had called the telephone company to do some work. After he arrived, she gave him a brief tour of the spring on the lower level – as many visitors ask to see. After he began working, Susan went to tell him she had to run an errand and would be back soon. It was almost lunchtime so the man asked if he could eat his lunch downstairs at the spring. Susan agreed and left for her errand. When she returned home the telephone man was sitting on the front porch. "I asked him how he enjoyed his lunch break. That's when he told me that about 5 minutes after I left, he stopped to have lunch down at the spring. He said he was almost finished eating when he heard me (he thought) come down the stairs and stand behind him. He commented what a nice place it was to eat lunch but received no reply. He then turned around to see who was standing there but found he was alone. He said he thought it was me because he was sure it was a woman's foot steps," said Susan.

Since she had not heard about the previous incidences, Susan quickly put it out of her mind. The next time something unusual occurred was a couple of years later when they were entertaining an overnight guest. A young woman from Alabama was considering finishing nursing school in Macon and was visiting the Bennetts. She was staying in the back guest room on the second floor that was formally the nursery. "The next morning she mentioned that I was certainly up late last night. She said she heard me (so she thought) walk down the hall and come to her door, pause, then walk away," said Susan. The young woman said it was definitely a woman's step. Susan knew she had gone to bed early but didn't want to frighten her guest. In fact, every time someone stays in that particular room they have a similar comment to share. Susan feels it must be Mamie still checking on the nursery once located there.

Susan claims to have seen Uncle Pliny once in 1994. She was painting a piece of furniture about eight o'clock one evening for a Macon Junior League charity auction. It was a 1950s dressing table with the tri-folding mirrors. She had pulled the dresser out into the second floor hallway for better light and had the mirror facing the back stairway. She had been working on the piece for some time and was hoping to take a break soon. She noticed a movement in the dresser mirror and glanced up to see a gentleman walking by that much resembled her husband in stature and coloring. She was on a roll and did not want to stop, so she asked him to bring her a diet soda. After about 45 minutes when she had not received it, she went down to Gilbert's office to see if he had forgotten her. "Gilbert said he had been working in his office since about 5:30 p.m. and hadn't even been upstairs. I knew then I had seen Uncle Pliny," she said.

Recently, Susan and Gilbert have been contacted by some of Uncle Pliny's descendants now residing in North Carolina. The relatives have provided them quite a few photographs of the home and a couple of snap shots of Pliny and Mamie. The most surprising finding was that Susan and Gilbert resemble Pliny and Mamie in stature. That may explain the several cases of mistaken identity.

Susan, Gilbert and their guests have all experienced cold

spots and heard unexplained sounds. However, Susan is quick to add that the spirits in the house are definitely friendly and no one has ever been frightened. "I think they want to have parties here again and that's why they are pleased with our restoration. We're glad they feel they can take part," she concluded.

SOURCES: Middle Georgia Archives, Washington Memorial Library, Macon, Georgia; *The Macon Telegraph*, "Spring's Source," 2/2/93.

* This location is a private residence and is not open to the public. Thank you for respecting the privacy of the current owners.

Photo Courtesy of Middle Georgia Archives, Washington Memorial Library, Macon, Georgia

1884 photo of the Academy of Music prior to the 1905 conversion to the Grand Opera House.

Chapter 2

"The Grand Lady of Mulberry"
Grand Opera House
Circa 1884
651 Mulberry Street

It was 2:25 in the morning and the theatre was completely empty. Yet there, floating soundlessly across the stage, was a woman in a white, iridescent flowing gown. The night watchman rubbed his eyes in disbelief. Were they playing tricks on him or could he be sure of what he had just seen?

Over a century ago in 1884, the Academy of Music opened its cultural doors to the residents of Macon. In 1905, major renovations took place and the theatre was renamed the Grand Opera House. An orchestra pit, chandeliers, balcony and box seats were added. Major acts, such as magician and world famous escape artist Harry Houdini, performed there regularly. Thousands were drawn to the playhouse, as it became a cultural mecca for theatrical and musical productions alike.

Since then, the Grand (as it is affectionately known) has endured triumph and tragedy. As the years passed, stage productions declined in popularity and cinema movies were shown. By the beginning of the 1960s, black and white televisions flickered in almost every home so the movies were discontinued. The year 1967, brought with it plans to demolish the structure and replace it with a high tech parking lot. Thank goodness, Val Sheridan and supporters of the Grand Opera House refused to let that happen. It was gloriously reopened in 1970 and even became the first building in Macon to appear on the National Register of Historic Places.

Shortly thereafter, the Grand suffered yet another devastating blow. *The Macon Telegraph* reported in the September 10, 1971, issue, that the managing director Randy Widner, was found dead from an apparent suicide in a room about 80 feet above the theatre stage. Widner had taken the management position just months earlier after an extensive theatrical career.

Many claim that some of the Grand's unusual occurrences can be attributed to Randy Widner. But strange activities have been documented there for years. In January 1937, night watchman J. D. Jones told *The Macon Telegraph* he saw a ghost floating across the stage the previous November.

Photo: Ken Krakow

Mid 1980's interior photo of the Grand Opera House.

"It was about 2:25 a.m. and I was about to make my rounds. I walked into the theatre and every thing was pitch black. And then I saw it. I am sure it was a woman. It was all dressed up in a long, glittery white gown like stage actresses wear. The image moved across the stage without a sound. It went to the wings, turned around and came back onto the stage and then started down one of the stair cases that led into the aisle I was standing in," said Jones.

He continued, "There wasn't any light in the theater that could have cause such a thing. I looked at the flashlight I carried to see if I'd accidentally turned it on, but I hadn't. I turned it on then and flashed it on her and – poof! She disappeared."

At the time of the ghost's alleged appearance, the theatre was not in use. Jones worked there for five years and had never seen the apparition before. "I still look for her too. Every time I go into the theatre to make my rounds, I've thought about that night and looked for the ghost. She's never come back. But I wouldn't be surprised some time if it showed up again," said Jones.

The night watchman was a professed country boy who had heard ghost stories all his life. But he had never actually witnessed anything until that night. In fact, prior to this event, he considered himself a nonbeliever in ghosts.

Jones recounted his fright and shock at the incident by saying, "Was I scared? My hair stood on end and my ears buckled while cold chills ran up and down my spine. Most anybody would have run, and I guess I would have too, but I don't believe I could have moved."

He said many people had come around the theater to ask him about it. "Most said they don't see how I could have seen anything in the dark and most just laugh at me. I wish they could have seen it."

Night watchman Jones is not the only one to say people have laughed over mysterious incidents at the Grand. More recently, local fireman Lt. Larry Smallwood has worked there during productions. He is aware of several accounts of strange activities and some have happened to him personally.

"One night I was down in front of the stage and began walking toward the back of the theater to pick up a copy of my schedule. As I walked down the aisle, I felt this cold air on my neck. It was really dark and all the lights were off. I walked a couple of steps and didn't think anything about it. Then I stopped. When I did, I heard two loud bangs up in the balcony. I knew no one was up there. That's when I took off. I went out into the lobby to the front door to leave but it was locked. When I tried to get my keys out to unlock it, the elevator opened up and one of the security guards stepped off. He said, 'What's after you?' and I said 'Nothing.' He said, 'No, I never seen a man with eyes that big that something wasn't after him.'"

Another time, Smallwood recalls after a musical ensemble production, he and several others were standing around chatting. He had just been upstairs to make sure all the doors were locked. He came through the balcony door and shut it. Nearby, he struck up a conversation with two small boys. All of a sudden the balcony door slammed shut behind him but he knew no one had walked by. Smallwood asked the boys who opened the door and they said it was some man. A check of the balcony found it empty. Smallwood claims he does not believe in ghosts. However, he has no explanation for his experiences or the stories he has heard about the Grand.

Rusty Banks, Technical Director for the Grand has also witnessed and heard tales of strange things happening there. "Last year about six of us were here working one afternoon doing a light hang. In order to 'fly' the lights we use a counter balance weight system. We loaded about 1,200 pounds on one end but the other end was empty. Something of equal weight has to be loaded on the other end before it will lift and make a balance. It's just like a child's seesaw. All of a sudden one end began to slowly rise off the stage floor but there was nothing on the other end to counter balance it! The other guys noticed what was happening and we were all in shock. After slowly rising several inches off the stage, the 1200 pound weight gently lowered back down without a sound. We were really surprised by that because no matter how softly we ever try to lower the weights, it's hard to set them down without a sound," Banks said. Out of curiosity, he mentioned that the six men who witnessed the event unsuccessfully attempted to pick up the 1200 pound weight. When they couldn't do it, they knew they had witnessed something unexplainable.

Another employee was attempting to change some light bulbs in one of the box seats a few years ago. Suddenly, he felt a cold breath as if someone was blowing on the back of his neck. At first he thought it was his imagination but it persisted. When he turned around to see what was causing it, the curtain to the box seat was gently swaying as if someone had just passed through it. The employee knew he was in the theatre alone.

One rainy Halloween night, part-time staff member Mike Seekins and another employee came to the Grand briefly to pick up some items. They were alone in the building.

While they were there, Mike thought Halloween would be an appropriate night to call out to any lingering spirits. In fun, he stepped onto the stage and loudly said, "Alright, it's Halloween! Where are y'all? What's up? Do something!" No sooner than he finished speaking, the rumbling began. He said it sounded like a herd of elephants racing across the floor above them. Needless to say they quickly left the building and Mike has not attempted to make contact since.

Besides all of these unusual occurrences, the Grand remains a historical, cultural asset to the community. After years of financial turmoil, another saving grace has come along for "The Grand Lady of Mulberry." In 1995, Mercer University leased it from Bibb County. The lease arrangement is scheduled to last twenty years. Mercer has agreed to continue to make the facility available to local groups that have traditionally used it. Hopefully, the Grand's curtain will continue to rise for future generations to come.

SOURCES: Middle Georgia Archives, Washington Memorial Library, Macon, Georgia; *The Macon Telegraph*, "Ghost in Theatre," 1/7/37; *The Macon Telegraph,* "Grand Listed As National Historic Site," 7/7/70; *The Macon Telegraph,* "Widner Named Director," 5/23/71; *The Macon Telegraph,* "Grand Managing Director Found Dead," 9/10/71; *The Macon Telegraph,* "Bibb Commission OK leasing of Grand to Mercer," 10/4/95.

Photo Courtesy of Middle Georgia Archives, Washington Memorial Library, Macon, Georgia

1960 photo of Fort Hawkins.

Chapter 3

"Birthplace of Macon"
Fort Hawkins
Circa 1806
Corner of Emery Highway and Maynard Street

A chill suddenly came over him, though the warm August night still held the thick humid feel of summer. As he glanced up at the fort's tower in the moonlight, he saw the cause for his uneasiness. There, still standing guard over Macon, was a soldier from over 192 years ago!

Is there a mysterious presence watching over Macon? Does the spirit of the soldier that once stood guard atop Fort Hawkins feel compelled to accomplish his assigned duty? Has the city of Macon thrived because someone has been watching out for her for almost two centuries? Area residents fortunate enough to have a piece of history right in their own backyard may be the best ones to answer.

Seeking information, I spoke recently with someone who was able to explain not only the birthplace of Macon but also some unusual activity occurring there.

In 1806, a huge struggle was underway for the possession and control of the extensive southeastern area of a newly discovered continent called America. It was then, seventeen years before the city of Macon was born, that Colonel Benjamin Hawkins, a U.S. Indian agent, came to this wilderness and established Fort Hawkins. Its strategic position was of great importance and aided in the protection of many early English settlers making their homes further up the coast. At that time, threats from the Spanish to the South, the French to the West and the Indians within the area were very prevalent and a constant worry to the early pioneers.

Built by the administration of President Thomas Jefferson, the fort overlooked the ancient Indian mounds now known as Ocmulgee National Monument. The area was then called Ocmulgee Old Field with the future site of Macon just across the Ocmulgee River. Located on a 100-acre reserve, the fort paved the way for the settlers who came in 1818. Though its basic role was protection, it also served as housing for ammunition and storage space.

The fort consisted of two large blockhouses (similar to the replica located there today) that were connected by a large, sturdy stockade type fence. The blockhouses were located at the southeast and northwest corner of the rect-

Artwork: Cindy Eversole

Diagram based on description of how Ft. Hawkins may have looked.

angular stockade. Both were 34 feet in height and were surmounted by eight-foot watchtowers. The first and second stories had portholes for cannon and musketry in the event of a skirmish. Frontiersman Daniel Boone would have been right at home!

Inside the connecting fence, four log cabins were used for storage of provisions, animal skins and soldiers' quarters. The officers' quarters were located in the center of the fort and surrounded by oak trees for shade. Approximately four acres were enclosed inside the stockade fence with 96 acres surrounding it. The outside acreage was cleared of undergrowth and large trees for better observation in hopes of preventing surprise attacks.

Benjamin Hawkins was sent to the area to ensure peace.

A former Revolutionary officer and a member of the Continental Congress, he served as a North Carolina Senator and was appointed by George Washington to negotiate with the Creek Indians. Many say Hawkin's friendly understanding was the key to his success. He is often said to have been one of the most successful peacemakers of the time. Many feel this is because he was governed by his heart and not his head.

The fort actually originated from a treaty between the United States and Creek Indians in 1805, at which time the Ocmulgee River became the southwestern boundary of the United States. Troops and militia organized there for years during Indian skirmishes and the War of 1812. In 1817, the last great assembly of Creek Indians occurred at the fort when 1,400 gathered to receive their annuities from the government. Settlers arrived and began making the land around the fort their home by 1818. A ferry was soon built across the Ocmulgee River and the area thrived. The settlement was called Fort Hawkins until the name of NewTown was adopted in 1821. Two years later as the city became more established, the name Macon was chosen.

In 1828, Fort Hawkins was decommissioned by the United States military. The fort's necessity had continued to decline, as the land grew more heavily populated. During the Civil War, the old fort was in ruins but was used as fortification against Union raids on the area. Twice in 1864, Union soldiers attempted to take Macon but both advances were repelled.

Photo Courtesy of Middle Georgia Archives, Washington Memorial Library, Macon, Georgia

1870's photo of Fort Hawkins.

The fort's ruins remained only a whisper of the past until 1938, when the Daughters of the American Revolution and the Works Progress Administration reconstructed a replica on the exact spot using some of the original basement stones. Since then, some say local officials have overlooked the fort's historical significance. In recent years, a Fort Hawkins Neighborhood Association has been formed and interest waxes and wanes. Thanks to the effort of local residents, school children are often able to visit the fort for a live lesson in history.

I spoke with a member of the Fort Hawkins Neighborhood Association who shared with me not only his love of the fort but also an unusual event he experienced. He asked not to be identified but believes that a kindred spirit may recognize his love of the fort.

"A few years ago, I contacted *The Macon Telegraph* to do an article about Fort Hawkins. The reporter and photographer said they would call me soon to meet them at the fort with the key. A few days passed and I forgot all about it until I was out in my yard one evening doing some watering. It was just getting dark. The city has placed spotlights on the fort and I happened to glance over at it. When I did, I saw a figure up in the top watchtower. My first thought was that the reporter or photographer from *The Macon Telegraph* was there to do the story. But then I realized the fort was locked and there was no way for anyone to get inside. Once inside, they would have to climb two ladders in the dark to reach the high watchtower. When I realized it was no one from *The Macon Telegraph* and that no one could possibly get inside, cold chills began to go down my spine. I rubbed my eyes to make sure I was not seeing something but the figure was still there. I could definitely tell it was a male but I could not make out a face or any details. He was looking towards the city as if he was on watch," he said.

"I truly believe what I saw was a kindred spirit of the fort. Whether it was Benjamin Hawkins or whoever, I know it is a presence and not an actual person. I have seen it a couple of other times when the light of a full moon rises over the fort. I am sure it is not my imagination. I've come to look for him at night when I pause to view the fort. I have never had any interaction with the so-called spirit world but I know there is something to this. A very peaceful feeling comes over me and I am sure it is a good spirit," he concluded.

Could this ghostly figure be a soldier still standing watch over the NewTown settlement now known as Macon? Was the soldier so devoted to his task in life that even in death he is compelled to make sure area residents are safe from harm? Regardless, Fort Hawkins still stands today as a proud reminder of Macon's past and promising future.

SOURCES: Middle Georgia Archives, Washington Memorial Library, Macon, Georgia; *The Macon Telegraph*, "Fort's Future" and "Macon First Settled Around Fort Hawkins," 9/26/93; *Historic Fort Hawkins Macon, Georgia* publication.

Photo: Ken Krakow

1998 photo of Lawrence Mayer Florist.

Chapter 4

"Doctor's Orders"
Hardeman-Mayer Building
Circa 1840s
608 Mulberry Street

*D*oors opening and closing by themselves, merchandise falling from secure locations and bells mysteriously jingling on their own. What could be the cause of this and other unusual activity at the recently renovated Lawrence Mayer Florist building downtown?

Gracing the city of Macon since cotton wagons rolled through town, this structure was formally known as the Concert Hall and later as the Hardeman Building. It played host to a variety of businesses over the last century and a half including Payne Apothecary Shop, Mix & Kirkland Bootery, Idle Hour Nursery & Florist and Young's Drug Store among others. Today's proud proprietors Lawrence and Jonathan Mayer, of Lawrence

Mayer Florist, have painstakingly restored the building in keeping with its graceful structure.

After visiting the area in the early 1980s, Lawrence Mayer was so captivated with the steamy, lush South that he moved here from Michigan in 1983. He set up shop on the corner of Second and Cherry Street and has since provided a floral flourish for much of Macon. With his overwhelming success came a growing business that was soon too small to fit its space.

After learning the nearby property at 608 Mulberry was available, Mayer researched its historical significance and was determined to again make it an asset to the community. He began renovations in 1994 and after a nine month delay and surviving a mammoth flood, he hosted a grand opening ceremony. Former Macon Mayor David Carter even presented him an official proclamation. In it, Carter praised Mayer for the returning of an invaluable gift to the city. The building was eventually listed with the National Historic Register and remains a feather in cap of Macon and Lawrence Mayer alike.

Take a drive by Lawrence Mayer Florist today and I am sure you would agree that he and Jonathan have achieved historical success. Recently, Lawrence Mayer sat down with me to share some interesting facts he discovered during the renovation process. He also hinted that some unusual things have happened there. When the location served as an apothecary shop, it apparently set the stage

Painting of Dr. Ambrose Baber made shortly before his untimely death in 1847.

for what may be causing many of the strange incidents that are occurring now.

Pharmacist G. Payne had been the builder and owner of the building back in the 1840s. He ran a bustling drug store in the location that filled most of the prescriptions for Macon and Middle Georgia residents. One doctor who sent many patients to Payne's Apothecary was Ambrose Baber. Some say during that time, Dr. Baber was one of the most respected physicians in the area.

Dr. Baber was originally from Virginia and served in the medical section of the U.S. Army during the War of 1812. A few years later he was drawn to Macon to practice medicine and enhanced the area greatly by participating in the establishment of the Macon we know today. Among his other contributions to the then pioneer town, he helped to found Christ Episcopal Church and was instrumental in setting aside a forest area for what is now Central City Park. Exotic plants and the study of botany were among Dr. Baber's passions and it was he who introduced the Chinese Magnolia and English Ivy that today enhances much of the downtown area.

In March of 1847, long before Cherry Blossoms bloomed in Macon, Dr. Baber was seeing one his patients, Leroy Jarrel. Jarrel had suffered from the complications of pulmonary disease, a chronic abscess, and a rapidly developing curvature of the spine. Dr. Baber wrote a prescription for him to relieve some of his afflictions and Jarrel took it to Payne Apothecary. Pharmacist Payne believed he detected an error and refused to fill it. The pharmacist warned the patient to consult with Dr. Baber. Sources say the doctor was enraged that the pharmacist would imply his prescription was inaccurate. He rushed into Payne's pharmacy and confronted him. After the pharmacist again refused to fill the prescription, Dr. Baber supposedly went behind the counter and filled it himself.

The doctor poured the solution he had made into a tumbler and drank it down without hesitation. He wanted to prove there was no error. "There is not enough sugar in it," Dr. Baber was reported to say. He then requested another lump. Before the pharmacist could hand it to him, the doctor made a feeble effort to loosen his cravat and open his vest, then fell to the floor dead. Nearby physicians rushed to his side but it was too late.

After his death, many strange incidents have occurred. Now that the Mayers have renovated the building, many witnesses are reportedly still spooked by some of their encounters.

"Often doors will automatically open or close all by themselves, especially in what was once the pharmacy area," said Mayer. "When people were working on the building to renovate it, they would be in the basement level and swear they saw someone at the other end. They would call out to the person thinking it was a co-worker but the figure would disappear."

Once employees witnessed a handblown glass Santa Claus mysteriously fall from the back of a shelf. It bounced repeatedly across the floor and finally came to a halt, still upright, and undamaged. "It seemed likely that after falling from a top shelf it might have been broken. But just like all the other things, you have to think about it," said Mayer.

Could the prideful doctor still be haunting the location of his death? Mayer said if they do have a presence, it is definitely a friendly ghost. Yet some employees still have their apprehensions. Several episodes have taken place upstairs on the second floor. Once an employee, Greg, was on the second floor when all of a sudden he heard a strange clicking noise behind him. He knew he was alone and nothing in the area should have caused the noise. When he turned around, several large potted artificial ficus trees were swaying to and fro as if a breeze were blowing. Greg said no windows were opened and the air conditioning was not on when the event occurred. He quickly went downstairs and to this day doesn't want to go back on the second floor.

Months later in the same area another employee, Jackie, was all alone tagging some merchandise. In the next room, she could hear the constant jingling of small metal bells. She knew that room housed a lot of the Christmas merchandise and that had to be the source of the sound. What Jackie didn't know is what would cause the bells to ring for such an extended period of time. As the noise continued, she bravely went about her task saying to herself that she was not going to let whatever was ringing those bells scare her.

Often, Mayer and employees have seen shadows or figures in their peripheral vision. When they turn their head to see what it could be, they find nothing there. Perhaps it's just the doctor whose great love of plants is drawing him back to investigate what type foliage Lawrence Mayer Florist has to offer.

SOURCES: Middle Georgia Archives, Washington Memorial Library, Macon, Georgia; *The Georgia Historical Quarterly*, March 1938.

Photo Courtesy of Middle Georgia Archives, Washington Memorial Library, Macon, Georgia

Photo of The Douglass Theatre marquee in the 1950's.

Chapter 5

"The Golden Screen"
The Douglass Theatre
Circa 1907
355 Martin Luther King, Jr. Blvd.

*A*udience members quietly murmured as they waited for the show to begin. Without warning, the theatre lights began mysteriously dimming at irregular intervals. At first, the audience thought it was the signal for show time. Many checked their watches as the shadowy cast glowed on and off. As it continued, even the staff members began to wonder what could really be causing such a strange phenomenon.

African-American entrepreneur Charles Henry Douglass was a visionary. In 1904, he embarked on a career that would forever alter the history of Macon. Combining his sense of real estate with his love of theatrical production, Douglass offered African-American citizens exciting business and entertainment opportunities.

Starting with the success of the Colonial Hotel, a pool-room, a soft drink counter and office spaces, Douglass soon expanded his operation to include theatrical entertainment. He opened the Douglass Theatre in 1921 and for a nickel, African American Maconites could enjoy three or four short films or an occasional vaudeville performance by well-known entertainers.

It has been said that The Douglass Theatre was modeled after Macon's Grand Opera House and definitely served its patrons well. The facility hosted early blues and jazz greats while running popular serials and feature-length films. The Douglass Theater proved to be a vital focal point for black entertainment for nearly half a century. The talents of Little Richard, Otis Redding and James Brown were even showcased there. Today, thanks to recent restoration efforts, The Douglass Theatre provides a rare glimpse of well-preserved African-American history for visitors and citizens alike.

Designed to reflect the Classical Revival style, Douglass set his theatre apart in the 1920s by paying attention to rich detail. The lobby boasted a ribbed vaulted ceiling and decorative ornamentation was abundant throughout. The entire theatre was enhanced by gold plaster trim molded into garlands of flowers, fruits, leaves and Nubian masks. The box seats were embellished with the appropriately monogrammed letters "CD." Perhaps The Douglass Theatre's most impressive quality was its gold fiber screen. In that day, such screens were more expensive than the

Mid 1920's photo of the interior of The Douglass Theatre.

more widely used white or silver screens. These legendary golden screens gave a warmer brownish gray effect to the films and were preferred by many audiences.

Apparently, Charles Douglass bestowed upon Macon the same affection he gave to his theatre. He has been called a prominent local philanthropist and an asset to the community. On December 6, 1978, *The Macon Courier* remembered Douglass as "the finest example of manhood to little boys of all races and in simple English, a great and famous man." Many realized that as Douglass' income grew, his charitable giving increased also. It is said no benevolent plea ever escaped his generous and prompt response. His life and works have been called a shining example for rising generations. Could this same man who so enthusiastically embraced life and his career be content to sit back and watch the current revival of The Douglass Theatre without making his presence known?

Painstaking restoration efforts have recently restored The Douglass Theatre to its former grandeur and offers visitors and citizens to Macon a glimpse of the past. In recent conversations with The Douglass Theatre staff, I felt the same devotion and excitement created by Charles Douglass many years ago. Chuck Phillips, Master Projectionist, has a special place in his heart for the theatre. His uncle, the late William Turner, also served as Master Projectionist at The Douglass for over 40 years. Turner's sister Mattie Turner Johnson played the piano for silent movies and raised Chuck Phillips from the age of five. "Mattie Johnson was my aunt but I considered her my mother because she raised me from such a young age," said Phillips. After growing up around The Douglass Theatre, Chuck Phillips spent 36 years with the Bibb County School System as an art teacher before recently retiring. He is staying busy these days operating the new state of the art computerized equipment in the projection room at The Douglass. In addition to the 70mm motion pictures and the 35mm movies, Phillips also coordinates the high-resolution video system, impressive laser shows, special effects lighting, a performance stage and supposedly the finest sound system in Georgia.

Phillips shared with me some unexplained episodes experienced since the theatre's reopening. "We have had quite a few unusual glitches and other frequent activity during the first year of our opening," said Phillips. He said several unexplained 'brown outs' have taken place with the electrical system. Phillips described a 'brown out' as when the lights dim to half their brightness. "They don't go completely out but it does create a brownish glow," he said.

Film projectors and curtains have also exhibited strange and repeated malfunctions. After the frequency of these events, Phillips said that he and the rest of the staff became convinced that Charles Douglass must be causing some of the commotion. They felt he must be proud of the renewed interest in the theatre and wanted to somehow be a part. "I took it a step further and started rubbing Mr. Douglass' statue on the head every morning for good luck and the hopes that everything would go well for the day," laughed Phillips.

The impressive bust of Charles Douglass that Phillips referred to is proudly displayed in the lobby of Douglass' beloved theatre. Crafted in 1995 by artist, Julie McCraney Brogdon, the sculpture is a noble tribute to a man who gave so much to Macon.

Upon his death in 1940, newspaper editorials reported, "The city has lost a valuable citizen in the death of Charles H. Douglass, Sr." Though Douglass is no longer with us, fortunately he has left a legacy for generations to come. His theatre remains an outstanding contribution to African American heritage and by chance if you visit The Douglass Theatre, Mr. Douglass just might welcome you there himself.

SOURCES: Middle Georgia Archives, Washington Memorial Library, Macon, Georgia; "The New Douglass Theatre Architectural History," Historic Preservation Services, Inc., 1994; The Douglass Theatre brochure & The Douglass Theatre fact sheet; *The Macon Courier* "Charles Henry Douglass, 1870-1940," 12/6/78.

Photo: Ken Krakow

1998 exterior photo of the former Allman Brothers Band home.

Chapter 6

"Ramblin' Man"
The Big House
Circa 1900
2321 Vineville Avenue

*I*t was almost midnight. In the dim glow of the television, the sleeping dogs suddenly sat up and began to growl. The house sitter knew no one was in the home except he and the owners three dogs. As the hairs began to stand up on the back of his neck, he realized the dogs were sensing a presence he could not see.

Perhaps the most recent claim to fame for this three-story English Tudor home would be its famous occupants from 1970-73, the Allman Brothers Band. But many don't realize the first owner of the home, Nathaniel Harris, also achieved notoriety. His recognition was gained through state and national, political and educational realms.

I found out quickly that Nathaniel Harris was himself a "Ramblin' Man." In the late 1800's he made his way across the Southeast doing good for many that crossed his path. He once said, "Georgia stretched out her arms to me when I had no home; she took me in when I was a wanderer, and since that day my heart has bent only in love and devotion to her."

A native of Tennessee, Harris was an attorney who served as the last ex-Confederate Governor of Georgia from 1915-17. He was one of the original founders of the Georgia School of Technology (Georgia Tech). He graduated with top honors from the University of Georgia in 1870. After the Civil War, Harris believed the South should never be second best in the industrial world again. He knew Georgia needed a school to produce technicians and engineers. Harris made his home in Macon and once even led a state-wide campaign to locate the Georgia School of Technology there.

Today, much of the unusual activity at the home probably stems from a female spirit of Nathaniel Harris' era. Current owners, Kirk and Kirsten West, have made the house not only their home, but also a memorial to the Allman Brothers Band. Kirsten sat down with me recently in the kitchen where many of the band's famous songs were written. I quickly realized there was much more to their story than just rock 'n roll.

Photo: Ken Krakow

1998 photo of the mysterious staircase.

In 1991, Kirk and Kirsten met through a personal ad in a Chicago entertainment weekly publication and within seven months they were married. Kirk serves as a road manager for the Allman Brothers Band. It was the first personal ad he had ever placed. Kirsten conveyed she had led a successful, yet unfulfilled life as a president of a Chicago company and the former wife of a conservative executive. When she saw the ad she thought Kirk might be the type man she needed. They clicked immediately and after marrying had the opportunity in 1994 to purchase and begin restoration on "The Big House."

Kirk had always been an avid collector of Allman Brothers Band memorabilia. He knew the house would make a great place to display his collection. The band had fondly nicknamed their hangout at 2321 Vineville Avenue, "The Big House." Now many of their cherished items would be returning.

The first strange experience Kirsten and Kirk had was a series of unusual accidents involving Kirsten. "I kept tripping and falling on the stairs. After one fall I had to stay in bed for three months because my back went out. I had a ruptured disk. Interestingly, I've spoken with the former owners of the home and the wife also experienced the same thing."

Kirsten is convinced that something has happened on the staircase. She pointed out an entire section of different spindles on the railing. The spindles have been replaced since the house was constructed and do not match the others. Oddly enough, they mark the spot where she repeatedly fell. She is not the only one who has fallen. Many claim to trip or feel as if they have been pushed from there.

Once Kirk and Kirsten were working with a film student from Atlanta on a documentary about the Allman Brothers Band. After they became friends, the girl spent the night in the home. The next morning as she was making her bed, she looked out onto a landing near her guest room. There she saw a door open by itself. She mentioned the experience to Kirsten and also related an unusual dream she had a few months earlier. The first time she visited the house, she went back to Atlanta and dreamt several times that she saw a woman running down the stairs of their home screaming.

Kirsten said her dogs, Martha (Little Martha), Liz (Elizabeth Reed) and Maggie always seem aware of things she and Kirk cannot see. They have a house sitter that once saw the dogs run up the stairs chasing a distinct shadowed form. The sitter says the thought of it still causes the hairs on the back of his neck to rise up.

Charles Olson, Kirsten's dad seems to have experienced the most peculiar of incidents. Before he passed away, Olson spent some time visiting the home. One morning, he said he got up early and dressed because he could smell cinnamon rolls baking, but no one had been near the kitchen. In fact, a music reporter for the *Chicago Sun Times* also stayed overnight and had the same aromatic experience.

Another morning, Kirsten's dad asked if she had been in his room the night before. She told him she had not. He had seen something standing by his bed. He swore it flew over him and then stood on the other side. A few days later he woke and said he saw someone lying above his bed in a reclined position. Her elbow was bent and her cheek was propped on her hand. He said she was wearing a bonnet and a long dress with ruffles from the neck to the waist. After he jumped out of the bed and stared at her for a few moments, she disappeared.

Also, annoying electrical disturbances have plagued the home and Kirsten mentioned that former residents have had priests over to bless the house. Often, ordinary household items seem to disappear. Twice she has lost her car keys only to find them both times on the floor under the middle of her bed. A former visitor to the home saw Kirsten in Atlanta. She asked Kirsten if they had experienced any key problems. The woman said that when she visited the home, keys often went missing. The keys would later turn up in some of the strangest places. Hairbrushes and toiletries have also disappeared only to show up a few days later in the spot where they belong.

Over the last few years, Kirsten and Kirk have done a great job restoring the home and its gardens. It is an ongoing project that takes immense patience. Regardless of the curious episodes, they are clearly happy there. "Who knows what's in store for us? This place has housed some other famous residents so maybe we will make our mark here too," she concluded.

SOURCES: Middle Georgia Archives, Washington Memorial Library, Macon, GA; *The Macon Telegraph*, "Dream House," 2/20/94; *The United Daughters of the Confederacy Magazine*, February, 1987, "Nathaniel Edward Harris: Last Ex-Confederate Governor of Georgia."

* This location is a private residence and is not open to the public. Thank you for respecting the privacy of the current owners.

1940's photo of the Ocmulgee National Monument.

Chapter 7

"The Lost City"
Ocmulgee National Monument
Circa 12,000 years ago
1207 Emery Highway

*H*orrendous shrieks split the frosty night air. The traders huddled closer around the warm campfire and pretended not to notice. They had often heard tales from local Indians about the Yamasee War waged at Ocmulgee in 1715. They had heard the tragic story of how the tribe's warriors were away fighting another battle when Carolina settlers attacked. Unfortunately, the only ones left in the Indian village were older people, women and children who were quickly brought down, defenseless in the attack. After the massacre, the place was deserted. The warriors would not go back because their sacred home was no more.

It has been said that there are ancient Indian Mounds along practically every large stream in Georgia. But yet these ancient ruins of the eastern United States are not nearly as well known as the rock art of the Pueblo Indians of the West. In fact, it was not until 1933 when "The Lost City" was officially excavated by the Smithsonian Institution, that the significance of Ocmulgee was finally realized.

Yet prior to that, many understood and respected the spiritual significance of this sacred land and its former inhabitants. In 1775, the following ghostly excerpt was recorded in James Adair's diary. Adair was a trader who often visited the area. It was he who heard stories from fellow traders and Indians that the Ocmulgee (originally meaning "bubbling water") Area was haunted: "Of most concern is the subject of their winter night's chat by the fire. Both they and several of our traders report very incredible and shocking stories. They will affirm that they have seen, and distinctly, most surprising apparitions, and heard horrid shrieking noises. They pretend it was impossible for all their senses to be deluded at the same time; especially at *Okmulge*. They strenuously aver, that when necessity forces them to encamp there, they always hear, at the dawn of the morning, the usual noise of Indians singing their joyful religious notes, and dancing, as if going down to the river to purify themselves."

For over two hundred years, this written documentation has existed of spirits who may remain at Ocmulgee. However, many don't realize that long before that, since pre-

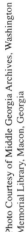

1930's photo of Ocmulgee National Monument excavation process.

9000 BC, inhabitants have lived in the Macon area along the Ocmulgee River. These first residents, Paleo-Indians, were nomadic hunters of large mammals and represent one of the earliest stages of human culture in North America. Long before our continent was even recognized, several Native American tribes had dwelled here including the: Archaic, Woodland, Early Mississippian, Late Mississippian and finally the Creek Indians. Many think that the first settlers to this great land were frontiersmen and women. However, we are only recent newcomers to the place we now call home. Thanks to the Ocmulgee National Monument, the mound builders ancient earth works still offer us a glimpse into the civilizations that once inhabited the eastern half of the United States. It was these ancient tribes who first established the Macon area as their home.

Eventually the Europeans did arrive and the Indians were pulled into the white man's world of politics and trade. Unfortunately, accompanying the Europeans innovative ideas and cultural advancements were disease, death and destruction. The Indians saw the collapse of their traditional way of life and lost all remains of the world they knew. And despite the fact that Ocmulgee is no longer inhabited, Creek Indians still consider it sacred ground.

Regardless of the Indians religious feelings for Ocmulgee, battle lines were drawn between North and South at the Mounds during the Civil War. Twice Union soldiers unsuccessfully attempted attacks on Macon. In 1864, what is now Ocmulgee National Monument was once the plantation home of Samuel F. Dunlap. "Sherman's March to the Sea" was underway and the offensive brought Union soldiers to Macon's doorstep. On July 30, 1864, "The Battle of Dunlap Hill" took place. Thankfully, there were no casualties. However, the battle is responsible for the cannonball that struck the home of Judge Asa Holt's home on Mulberry Street, better known today as "The Cannonball House." Union soldiers had aimed the cannon at the then Confederate treasurer William Butler Johnston's home (Johnston-Felton-Hay House). Instead, the cannonball landed a few doors down at Judge Holt's residence.

After the Civil War, the Mounds were sadly overlooked

for years while people were allowed to scavenge the area for arrowheads and pieces of pottery. Macon thrived and in time focused on its future instead of its past. Finally in the 1930s, after years of neglect, archeologists from the Smithsonian Institution conducted at Macon what was probably one of the most extensive excavations to date in the history of the country. They uncovered evidence of cornfields, a village site, prehistoric trenches, a funeral mound, fences, a trading post and a ceremonial building. Federal preservation efforts began and finally the Ocmulgee National Monument was officially established in 1936.

Since then, employees and visitors to the park have experienced some eerie things similar to what trader James Adair reported in 1775. Could unsettled spirits from the past still linger on this sacred ground which is located only a mile and a half from downtown Macon?

A couple of years ago, after a busy day at the monument, Sam Lawson, a former park ranger, was locking up the Visitor Center: "A woman with a group of kids had just left and I was checking the building. She took the kids and went out the front door. I locked it behind her. As I continued closing doors and turning out lights I heard a child laugh. It was a mischievous laugh like 'I'm hiding and you can't find me.' Knowing that the children had just been in the building, I thought I must have locked one in here."

After a complete search of the building, Lawson found no one. Sylvia Flowers, master ranger, was outside locking things up. "I asked her if she'd come inside and help me find the child. We looked in closets and unlocked doors and looked everywhere we could imagine. Absolutely nothing turned up. We didn't know what to do. Sylvia asked me if I was sure I had heard someone. She joked with me that I must have been hearing things," said Lawson.

A couple of weeks later the staff was having lunch together and several of them started poking good-hearted fun at Lawson about the incident. "The woman who was the gift shop manager looked at me very strangely but didn't say anything. Later, she came to me and asked where I had heard the child's laughter. When I told her she said she had been closing up about the same time one day and came through that area and heard it also. She said her daughter was with her so they both searched the building but found no one. Something unusual apparently happens in that particular section of the building but I am not sure what it is," Lawson remarked.

When I visited the monument recently, master ranger Sylvia Flowers shared with me not only some of the history surrounding the Monument but some of it's legends and stories as well. "Through the years, there have been reports of people seeing a white dog and a black dog around the grounds," Flowers said.

In our conversation, Sam Lawson implied that the small white dog has supposedly been seen around the old Dunlap residence. Many have mentioned approaching the dog only to have it disappear before they reach it. It is said Samuel Dunlap owned a small white dog that stayed in the yard near his home. Could this white dog be one and the same?

To the Creek nation today, legend has it that the spirit of a large black dog is left behind to guard ancient ceremonial areas like Ocmulgee. On numerous occasions, staff and visitors to the park have noted such sightings. Is this large black dog there guarding the Earth Lodge Mound that once served as a gathering place for religious and political ceremonies thousands of years ago?

Once when a group was touring the grounds one night during a Cherry Blossom Lantern Light Tour, one woman witnessed a peculiar sight. It was very foggy and while the group was waiting, one of the women at the back of the line thought she spotted a tall, slender man. He was wearing what seemed to be a grayish suit and a cowboy hat. He was walking through the mist at a distance. The episode upset her so badly that she called the park staff the next day to verify that it had been one of their staff members dressed as a Confederate soldier. Unfortunately, the staff was unable to confirm what she had witnessed because none of them had been dressed in that particular attire or had seen any of the visitors fitting that description.

Regardless of the stories and legends that now surround the sacred land we know as Ocmulgee National Monument, it still remains a vital yet often overlooked part of Macon history. Master park ranger Sylvia Flowers sums it up best when she says the mounds are just one chapter in the saga of the history surrounding Middle Georgia. "I tell kids history is not about dates. It's about people," said Flowers. Who knows, maybe some of those former inhabitants are still hanging around until we get the message.

SOURCES: Middle Georgia Archives, Washington Memorial Library, Macon, Georgia; *Adair's History of the American Indians*, Samuel Cole Williams, 1930; "Mound Builders," National Parks Magazine, January/February, 1993; *The Macon Telegraph*, "Lucky Ones Recall Lean Times," 11/13/83; "Old Ocmulgee Fields," Georgia Educational Journal; "Omulgee – Mysteries of the Mounds," 1997 Video.

Photo: Ken Krakow

1998 photo of the former Beall's 1860 restaurant.

Chapter 8

"The Columns"
Beall's
Circa 1860
315 College Street

𝒞 ould ghosts be naturally attracted to empty locations where they find themselves less likely to be disturbed? Or do they prefer living occupants to witness their ghoulish performances?

Currently, no inhabitants are available to witness any usual happenings at 315 College Street but past residents and visitors to the home have had their fair share. Cold spots, blinking lights, strange noises and a mysterious discolored marking all add up to unusual but harmless phenomena.

Built in 1860, the home has always served as a focal point for entertaining. Its massive fourteen foot ceil-

ings, wide doorways, double parlors and monumental staircase add up to a spectacular social setting. When Nathan
Beall built the original Georgian style frame structure, he
had already amassed a fortune as a cotton plantation owner
and cotton broker.

Soon the war between the states erupted and circumstances
caused the home to change hands many times. Could this
constant upheaval have made unsettled spirits attempt to
make their permanent home there?

In 1901, war hero and civic leader, Captain Sam Dunlap
transformed the house into an elaborate Greek Revival
Mansion. He added eighteen impressive Corinthian columns that surround the front and both sides. Those columns have made the home a beloved Macon landmark ever
since.

Eventually, Mr. and Mrs. R.V. Lassiter purchased the location in the 1940s and affectionately nicknamed their
palace "The Columns." The Lassiters loved to entertain
and the home continued its fine tradition for luncheons,
dinners and other lavish affairs. The home was not a restaurant at that time but Mrs. Lassiter did arrange reserved
events for special parties. "The Columns" soon became
the toast of the town and the Lassiters filled it with parties
and laughter for many years.

The Lassiters eventually sold the home in 1967. Soon after in 1969, The Allman Brothers Band used the porch as

Beall's as it appeared as a private residence in the 1940's.

an interesting backdrop for the cover of their first album. Glaring back at the camera, clad in bell-bottoms, they posed beside one of the gigantic columns. At that moment, they gave a face to what would become known in the music industry as Southern Rock. Sadly, by then, the house was badly in need of repair and had fallen victim to vandals. Missing marble mantels, peeling paint and broken windows spoke of neglect but the true character of the home still showed through.

Thankfully, during the 1970s and 80s, the landmark was remodeled and has served as the site for several restaurants. Steak, lobster and southern cuisine have since been served from the same kitchen where Mrs. Lassiter once prepared her famous Thursday night smorgasbords for the "Who's Who" of Macon.

It has been the staff and customers of these restaurants who in the last two decades have relayed most of the eerie stories. I spoke with one former employee who believed many of the tales were contrived to draw business. He did say however that a certain room upstairs remained unusually chilly.

According to area ghost author, Barbara Duffey, in her 1995 book entitled *Banshees, Bugles and Belles* the ghosts at Beall's Restaurant were often busy. In her book she relates, "On one occasion in 1994 the 12th Georgia Brigade of Confederate re-enactors, wearing their full-dress uniforms, dined in the upstairs banquet hall. During the dinner, the lights on each of the two huge antique brass chandeliers flickered off and on in sequence-first one, then next until they were all flickering at various intervals. This would be an impossible feat to accomplish by hand, because both chandeliers are controlled by the same switch and wired to turn on and off simultaneously. The display both dazzled and baffled everyone in the room. They wondered if the prank was caused by the spirit of someone who had lived in the house who might have been a member of the original 12th Georgia Brigade, a unit comprised primarily of Macon men."

In the Beall House chapter, Barbara Duffey also writes, "On another night, a waiter was fixing drinks in the upstairs bar when the ice cubes began to pop out of the glasses, like popcorn hopping out of a hot pan. He tried to put the cubes back into the glasses, but they continued to pop out in a frightening display. Frantic, he left the room vowing never to return again. At the same bar on another busy night, a bartender noticed a young girl dressed in a long white gown sitting quietly on one of the stools. He turned around to get a soda, and when he looked back the girl had disappeared. No one working that night could remember seeing anyone fitting the girl's description."

In October of 1997, *The Macon Telegraph* listed the Beall House as one of their "Favorite Haunts" in a Halloween tribute. The article stated, "Even though Beall's 1860 restaurant has closed, there is still a stain there that won't go away. It's a spot near the building where legend has it a young woman threw herself out of the second story window to her death."

Who was this young woman who supposedly ended her life at the Beall house all too soon? That is one answer my research has failed to uncover. Is she just a ghostly myth or is this remaining stain a cruel reminder of her death? Former restaurant staff members say they often scrubbed the stain to no avail.

Several years ago upon moving to Macon, an acquaintance mentioned the restaurant and its ghostly inhabitants to me. One playful spirit was even known to occasionally pinch restaurant patrons. They said silverware, glasses and plates never seemed to cooperate while the wait staff was setting up for large parties.

Bill Lucado, current owner, says maybe no one will ever know just who or what still lingers at 315 College Street. However, one thing is certain, at the time of publication the property is currently on the real estate market and who-ever is lucky enough to purchase it will definitely own a charming relic of Macon's past.

SOURCE: Middle Georgia Archives, Washington Memorial Library, Macon, Georgia; *Banshees, Bugles and Belles: True Ghost Stories of Georgia*, 1995, Barbara Duffey; *The Macon Telegraph*, "Aging Mansion Waiting on Fate," 1/14/72; *The Macon Telegraph*, "Preservation at Its Best," 10/28/73; *The Macon Telegraph*, " Favorite Haunts," 10/28/97.

Photo: Ken Krakow

1998 exterior photo of the City Auditorium.

Chapter 9

"Pride of Macon"
City Auditorium
Circa 1925
Corner of First Street and Cherry Street

$\mathcal{T}$he shadowed form hovered several seconds under the archway. The two men watched in awe as the grayish mist slowly floated down the stairs and into the aisle between the seats. Then it quickly vanished leaving the men uncertain of what they had just witnessed.

Guy E. Paine once hailed it the "Pride of Macon." For years, the city had dreamed of an entertainment, cultural and sporting arena. In 1925, extensive plans for the limestone, Greek revival, fire proof, $600,000 building became a reality. Designed by architects Egerton Swartwout of New York and Dennis & Dennis of Macon, it was the talk of the town. Every citizen was proclaimed a stockholder and had been assured their tax dollars were being well spent.

At the time of its completion, the new auditorium was roofed with the largest copper cover dome in the world. Not many Georgia cities could boast of an entertainment center that was the size of the Pantheon in Rome surrounded by forty massiye Doric columns.

It all began in 1916 when municipal authorities saw the need and started a movement to secure the building's future. Bond issues were passed over the next couple of years and a temporary wooden structure was erected in 1918. The Chamber of Commerce decided to appoint a committee in 1920 to see what could be done to ensure that the project would be completed. Their first action was to submit a survey to 140 other Chambers of Commerce to see if other communities had confronted the same issues. The committee was eager to see what prospects they were facing. Various methods of financing were also discussed and a six percent sales tax was eventually imposed for six years. Its purpose was to fund the $600,000 building project.

Eventually, the architects were selected and plans were underway. In an article appearing in the June 1924 issue of a Middle Georgia publication, Guy E. Paine said, "At the opening gathering you will see an audience of 4,000 people, your neighbors and friends from right here in Macon, all seated in a great circular room under a domed

1918 photo of the temporary civic structure built prior to the City Auditorium construction in 1925.

ceiling seventy feet high, the entire place brilliantly lighted and affording a beautiful and harmonious spectacle, and you hear the strains of music from the great organ. You will be proud of your auditorium."

Several years prior to Paine's statement, *The Macon Telegraph* published an article relating the history of the site of the proposed City Auditorium at the corner of First and Cherry Streets. Before the civil war they reported that a lumberyard and planing mill were on the lot. After fighting between the states erupted, the location became a match factory and patriotic metal depository used in the manufacturing of cannons.

"It was a crude and clumsy match, but it struck fire

alright, and was about the only match used in Macon. Even these had no tremendous sale, for there were many families unable to afford them. They covered the coals at night with ashes for the fires in the morning," reported *The Macon Telegraph*, February 25, 1917.

The Macon Telegraph article stated, "The yard connected with the planing mill was used as a receiving dump for the contributions from patriotic people in the way of copper and brass made into the many shapes to be seen in every house before the war, such as brass candlesticks, doorknobs and knobs of andirons, fenders, candlesnuffers, stairrods, keys, copper kettles and other vessels. Churches and schools gave up their bells, and all of them were melted into cannons at Findlay's foundry, then the Confederate arsenal."

It was said that much of the metal remained on the lot after the war. One bell left behind had been donated by a church in Rome, Georgia. Several decades later, the Ocmulgee Fire Company was building it's No. 2 volunteer firehouse in the middle of First Street at the intersection of Cotton Avenue. One night, in a harmless prank, several volunteer fire fighters were believed to have swiped the bell for their new engine house.

Originally, the chosen lot was a huckleberry swamp that reached from the river to about the corner of Poplar and Cotton Avenue. An old federal stagecoach road that was built from logs ran through the swamp. Stagecoaches start-

1969 interior photo of the City Auditorium.

ing from New York and New Orleans passed over the road that in time became Cotton Avenue.

Since its establishment, the City Auditorium has served as a focal point for the area's most entertaining events. Frequent concerts, dances, tradeshows and conventions are just a few of the functions taking place for audiences of up to 2,600 people. Today the facility is still indeed a proud monument to a Macon past and future. Thousands have passed through its doorways and some may even remain.

A few years ago, I spoke with several former employees of the facility who said many often hear things in the building at night when it was suppose to be empty. Distinct sounds of former parties and gatherings can be heard. Music, the murmuring of voices and echoing footsteps have caught many employees off guard. Often they have checked the building only to find it completely empty.

One former employee, who declined to be identified, reported that he and another person once witnessed a strange spectacle. They were on the lower level and happened to look up into the balcony area. There, in one of the domed shaped entrances they saw a dark distinctive shadow or mist. It glided from the opening down an isle into one of the rows where it lingered for a moment. They then saw it slowly float away. Neither claim to believe in so called ghosts and spirits but both were sure what they saw. Could former visitors to the auditorium actually have had such a wonderful time that they decided to remain in the building reliving endless theatrical productions, parties, dances or even sporting events?

The next time you attend an event at the City Auditorium, take heed and remember, you just may want to check the people sitting around you. They may not necessarily be the ones you came with.

SOURCES: Middle Georgia Archives, Washington Memorial Library, Macon, Georgia; National Register of Historic Places Inventory – Nomination Form, 1970; *The*

Macon Telegraph, "Site for City Auditorium Figures in Civil War History," 2/ 25/17; Middle Georgia publication, "New Auditorium to be Pride of Macon," June 1924.

Photo: Ken Krakow

1998 exterior photo of Walker and Suzan Rivers home.

Chapter 10

"Parlor Tricks"
Rivers Home
Circa 1879
923 High Street

$\mathcal{M}$ysterious sounds and ghostly apparitions occasionally visit the home of Walker and Suzan Rivers on High Street. The Rivers are more curious than frightened but still wonder what could be causing such unusual phenomena.

Originally, High was a street of prestige and distinction, formerly referred to as the "Hill." Property owners included prominent doctors, attorneys, financial wizards, mayors, political representatives, military officers, a railroad president, bankers and a cotton broker. The half-acre lots first sold in 1838 for about $400.00 each and were considered prime Macon real estate.

The street was originally 120 feet wide. It was laid out

in the first city survey as an extension of Plum Street. In 1863, the park area was established in the middle and both sides officially became known as High Street. Today it is still considered home to many families, St. Joseph's Catholic School, the Sidney Lanier Cottage and a few other restless spirits.

In 1840, the birthplace of Sidney Lanier was constructed and sat astride one of the High Street lots. Eventually, the land was divided into two parcels. The Sidney Lanier Cottage was moved to one portion and the other portion was sold in 1879 to a successful businessman named William Burden. Burden began his career as a clerk in the dry goods business and over the course of twenty years became a partner in Coleman, Burden & Solomon. He was a well respected citizen who eventually went into banking and became the father of seven children.

"We believe a Queen Anne Victorian style home was built on the lot in 1879 by William Burden," said current owner Walker Rivers. Walker and his wife Suzan purchased the home in 1996 and have since encountered some strange activity. When I visited with them recently, they were eager to share the historical and unusual events surrounding 923 High Street.

While there, I learned that Burden sold the home to a Walter Stevens who purchased it as a wedding gift for his daughter and her new husband, Dr. Maury M. Stapler. They completely changed the outside structure of

Photo: Ken Krakow

1998 photo of the front parlor where a party can still be heard.

the home in 1903 to the then popular Greek Revival style. The house was perfect for entertaining and the Staplers enjoyed having people into their home.

Sometime between the 1930s and 40s, the home was converted into apartments. Many people lived there through the years but it was Dr. William K. Jordan and his family who decided to stay. They purchased the home in 1951 and remained there until the Rivers moved in recently with their three young daughters.

"One of the most unusual things about the house is that several people have heard the distinct sounds of a party while they are in the front parlor," said Suzan. None of the people who heard it knew that others had the same sensation. She continued, "We've had three different people from various backgrounds: an electrical engineer, a teacher and a college graduate. They all tell us the same thing. They are not the typical individual who would believe in ghosts but they are convinced of what they heard."

The first couple of times this happened, Walker and Suzan thought maybe the Sidney Lanier Cottage next door was hosting a party. Each time, a quick glance out the window told them otherwise. "We checked over there and it was completely dark," said Walker. Could this have been traces of a past party replaying itself in full swing?

Occasionally, an elderly man in a white terry cloth bathrobe has been spotted wandering around the home. Once when Suzan's nephew was sleeping over, he had an actual encounter with him. "My nephew asked us who the man was. We had no idea what he was talking about. He had spent the night in a sleeping bag on the first floor. He said he awoke and the gentleman was standing over him looking down as if he wondered who the boy was," said Suzan.

Since moving into the home, the Rivers have been slowly piecing together its history. They have conducted some extensive research and have spoken with several people who have been very helpful. During the course of their investigation, they uncovered that one of the Burden's seven children died in the house. However, they were unable to determine why. A couple of weeks went by and Suzan woke up in the middle of the night after a strange dream. She told Walker she knew why the girl passed away. She said the dream revealed that the girl's death had something to do with poison. Walker didn't think much about it until he was in the Middle Georgia Archives at the Washington Memorial Library a couple of weeks later. He ran across the Burden girl's obituary in the Sunday, August 15, 1886 edition of *The Macon Telegraph*.

Along with her funeral notice he found a small article explaining her death. It said, "Miss Annie Burden, daughter of Mr. W. H. Burden of the firm Coleman, Burden & Solomon died at her father's residence on High Street yesterday morning at 4 o' clock of typhoid fever."

The article continued that about a month before she had been visiting her relatives on their farm in Newnan, Georgia. "After returning from a long walk over the field she bathed her face and hands in cold water. She eventually began having fevers but they were not considered severe. Soon afterward she swallowed some iodine by mistake, which made her quite sick. She came home not fully recovered from the effects of the mistake. Dr. Holt was called in and it was found she was suffering from typhoid fever." The article noted that Miss Burden was 17 years of age and was in the junior class of Wesleyan Female College. Could Suzan's dream have been correct? Was Annie Burden's episode of typhoid fever aggravated by her deadly miscalculation of ingesting poisonous iodine?

Walker has also had some unusual experiences in the house. "Once I was in the kitchen and out of the corner of my eye, I know I saw a low, dark shadow go past the door that leads into the hallway. I knew it wasn't one of the kids or the dogs. They weren't even around when it happened," he said.

One night recently, Walker said he was coming downstairs when he heard the front door shut. He wondered who it could be because the door was locked. He saw a shadow cross the floor at the bottom of the stairs in the foyer. He thought it was Suzan's nephew who also lives in the house. He saw the shadow as it quickly passed and went in the direction of the downstairs bathroom. He heard the bathroom door close. Shortly the nephew actually did arrive. Walker knew then he must have heard someone else go into the bathroom. If it had not been the nephew, who was it? They both decided to checked the bathroom door and found it closed. When they knocked and opened the door, the bathroom was empty. "Usually this door always stays open and I knew it wasn't Suzan or the girls because they were upstairs," Walker said.

Sounds of footsteps and other unexplained noises are often heard at the Rivers home. However, they have no real explanation and say they are very comfortable living there.

In the brief time since they have owned the home they have

held several large parties and even a family wedding. They love to entertain and are apparently exceptional hosts. Maconites already rave about the Rivers newest tradition, an annual New Year's Eve party. Perhaps if you ever score an invitation to this or any future event at the Rivers, you can check out the front parlor for yourself. Maybe you'll catch a glimpse of a prior resident enjoying the festivities.

SOURCES: Middle Georgia Archives, Washington Memorial Library, Macon, Georgia; *The Macon Telegraph*, "Death of Miss Burden," 8/15/1886.

* This location is a private residence and is not open to the public. Thank you for respecting the privacy of the current owners.

About the Author

Mary Lee Irby moved to Macon, Georgia in 1992 and quickly became fascinated with its intriguing architecture and rich history. She is currently the Communications Director for United Way of Central Georgia. Mary Lee is a graduate of Valdosta State University and is originally from Cordele, Georgia. She resides in Macon with her husband Robert Edward Irby.

Know Any Area Ghost Stories?

Do you have any interesting ghost stories about the area
that you'd like to share?
Contact author Mary Lee Irby at the address below:

Mary Lee Irby
c/o Vestige Publishing Company
P.O. Box 13726
Macon, GA 31208-3726

Stories based on historical facts, legends, folklore or
personal experience will be considered for future
publications. The author will honor all requests
for confidentiality.

Mary Lee Irby ————————————————————

At Right: *'Birdseye Map of Macon - 1887*
Courtesy of Middle Georgia Archives,
Washington Memorial Library,
Macon, Georgia

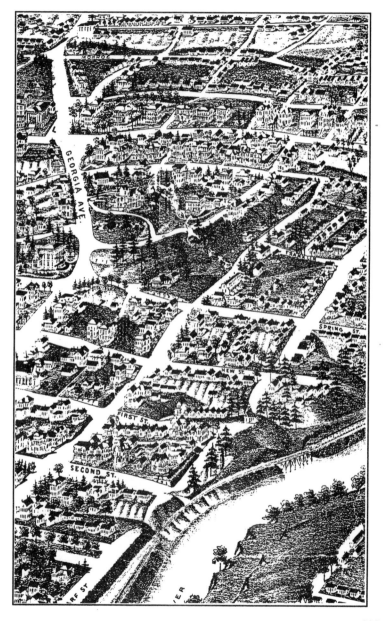